GEMINI

HOROSCOPE

& ASTROLOGY

2022

Published by Mystic Cat Press

Suite SM-2380-6403

14601 North Bybee Lake Court

Portland, Oregon 97203

Phone: +1 (805) 308-6503

SiaSands@hotmail.com

Contents

January 16

February 24

March 32

April 40

May 48

June 56

July 64

August 72

September 80

October 88

November 96

December 104

GEMINI 2022
HOROSCOPE & ASTROLOGY

Four Weeks Per Month

Week 1 – Days 1 - 7

Week 2 – Days 8 - 14

Week 3 – Days 15 - 21

Week 4 – Days 22 – Month-end

GEMINI

Gemini Dates: May 21st to June 20th
Zodiac Symbol: Twins
Element: Air
Planet: Mercury
House: Third
Colors: Yellow, blue

2022 AT A GLANCE

Eclipses

Partial Solar – April 30th

Total Lunar – May 16th

Partial Solar – October 25th

Total Lunar -November 8th

Equinoxes and Solstices

Spring - March 20th

Summer - June 21st

Fall – September 23rd

Winter – December 21st

Mercury Retrogrades

January 14th, Aquarius - February 4th Capricorn

May 10th, Gemini - June 3rd, Taurus

September 10th, Libra - October 2nd Virgo

December 29th, Capricorn - January 1st, 2023, Capricorn

2022 FULL MOONS

Wolf Moon: January 17th, 23:48.

Snow Moon: February 16th, 16:57

Worm Moon March 18th, 07:17

Pink Moon: April 16th, 18:54

Flower Moon: May 16th, 04:13

Strawberry Moon: June 14th, 11:51

Buck Moon: July 13th, 18:37

Sturgeon Moon: August 12th, 01:35

Corn, Harvest Moon: September 10th, 09:59

Hunters Moon: October 9th, 20:54

Beaver Moon: November 8th, 11:01

Cold Moon: December 8th, 04:07

THE MOON PHASES

New Moon (Dark Moon)

Waxing Crescent Moon

First Quarter Moon

Waxing Gibbous Moon

Full Moon

Waning Gibbous (Disseminating) Moon

Third (Last/Reconciling) Quarter Moon

Waning Crescent (Balsamic) Moon

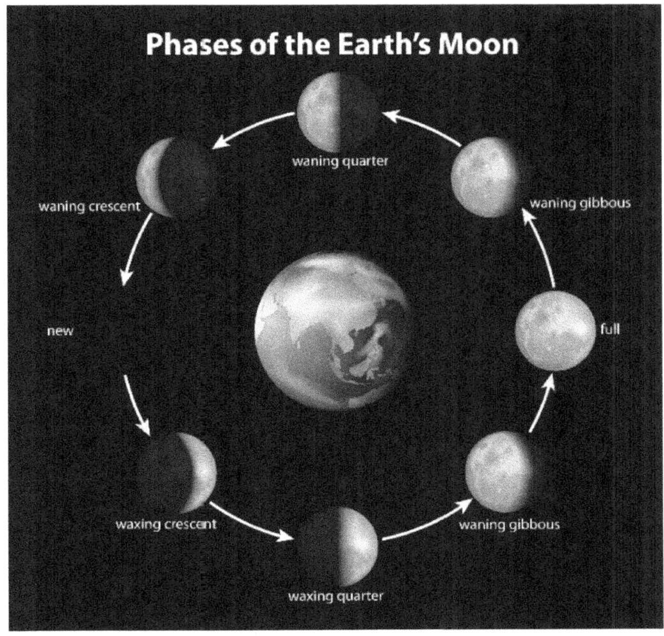

2022

JANUARY

M	T	W	T	F	S	S
					1	2
3	4	5	6	7	8	9
10	11	12	13	14	15	16
17	18	19	20	21	22	23
24	25	26	27	28	29	30
31						

FEBRUARY

M	T	W	T	F	S	S
	1	2	3	4	5	6
9	10	11	12	11	12	13
14	15	16	17	18	19	20
21	22	23	24	25	26	27
28						

MARCH

M	T	W	T	F	S	S
	1	2	3	4	4	6
7	8	9	10	11	12	13
14	15	16	17	18	19	20
21	22	23	24	25	26	27
28	29	30	31			

APRIL

M	T	W	T	F	S	S
				1	2	3
4	5	6	7	8	9	10
11	12	13	14	15	16	17
18	19	20	21	22	23	24
25	26	27	28	29	30	

MAY

M	T	W	T	F	S	S
						1
2	3	4	5	6	7	8
9	10	11	12	13	14	15
16	17	18	19	20	21	22
23	24	25	26	27	28	29
30	31					

JUNE

M	T	W	T	F	S	S
		1	2	3	4	5
6	7	8	9	10	11	12
13	14	15	16	17	18	19
20	21	22	23	24	25	26
27	28	29	30			

JULY

M	T	W	T	F	S	S
				1	2	3
4	5	6	7	8	9	10
11	12	13	14	15	16	17
18	19	20	21	22	23	24
25	26	27	28	29	30	31

AUGUST

M	T	W	T	F	S	S
1	2	3	4	5	6	7
8	9	10	11	12	13	14
15	16	17	18	19	20	21
22	23	24	25	26	27	28
29	30	31				

SEPTEMBER

M	T	W	T	F	S	S
			1	2	3	4
5	6	7	8	9	10	11
12	13	14	15	16	17	18
19	20	21	22	23	24	25
26	27	28	29	30		

OCTOBER

M	T	W	T	F	S	S
					1	2
3	4	5	6	7	8	9
10	11	12	13	14	15	16
17	18	19	20	21	22	23
24	25	26	27	28	29	30
31						

NOVEMBER

M	T	W	T	F	S	S
	1	2	3	4	5	6
7	8	9	10	11	12	13
14	15	16	17	18	19	20
21	22	23	24	25	26	27
28	29	30				

DECEMBER

M	T	W	T	F	S	S
			1	2	3	4
5	6	7	8	9	10	11
12	13	14	15	16	17	18
19	20	21	22	23	24	25
26	27	28	29	30	31	

Time set to Coordinated Universal Time Zone

(UT±0)

Meteor Showers are on the date they peak.

JANUARY

Sun	Mon	Tue	Wed	Thu	Fri	Sat
						1
2	3	4	5	6	7	8
9	10	11	12	13	14	15
16	17	18	19	20	21	22
23	24	25	26	27	28	29
30	31					

ASTROLOGY

January 2nd - New Moon in Capricorn 18:33

January 3rd - Quadrantids Meteor Shower. January 1st-5th.

January 7th - Mercury at Greatest Eastern Elongation

January 9th - First Quarter Moon in Aries 18:11

January 14th - Mercury Retrograde begins in Aquarius

January 17th - Wolf Moon. Full Moon in Cancer 23:48

January 25th - Last Quarter Moon Scorpio 13:42

NEW MOON

FULL MOON

JANUARY WEEK ONE

The Quadrantids Meteor Shower blazes across the night sky this week. Opportunities ahead illuminate fantastic potential. It brings the magic into your life and lets you charge forward towards new adventures. Synchronicity guides the path and creates a shift for your emotions that harmonizes and balances energy. It's an environment that encourages creativity to thrive. A serendipitous route connects you with a personal vision. It fuels options that improve your social life.

Things are ready to shift forward soon. Something you hope for does reach fruition. It allows you to broaden your horizons. It releases restrictions and brings essential adjustments that help you crack the code to a new and enterprising path forward. It takes you towards an optimistic chapter that lets you expand your abilities into new areas. It creates space to nurture your talents and reap the rewards of expansion.

Waves of potential draw rejuvenation. It lets you put on your rebel's cap and forge an adventurous path towards developing a creative enterprise. It brings a phase of liberation, freedom, and growth that clears the slate and reboots the potential possible. Mingling and networking with kindred spirits bring a dynamic, harmonious, and abundant phase for your social life. Fresh winds of possibility blow change into your world.

JANUARY WEEK TWO

Mercury Retrograde begins in Aquarius at the week's end. There are delays with reaching your destination. It does come together over time, but because of influences outside of your direct control, you will have to delay plans until you get the go-ahead. The red light switches to green in due course, bringing excitement and adventure. You discover room to spread your wings and fly towards developing your social life. It brings a breakthrough that opens the door to an abundant landscape.

Incorporating lessons of the past wipe the slate clean. It kickstarts a new area. Information is imminent that paves the way forward. It underscores your desire for change and stability. It unlocks a gateway towards growth and prosperity as it helps you capture the missing element in your life. Small changes draw substantial benefits. Creating actual progress brings the chance to dive into a new area of interest.

Expect improvement in personal growth areas; this lets you embrace developing better social connections. It breathes fresh air into your surroundings and draws rejuvenation. The tides turn in your favor; it brings a chance to unwind in a social environment. Lively discussions, sharing thoughts, ideas, and memories, let you pack a chapter brimming with well-being.

JANUARY WEEK THREE

The Wolf Moon. Full Moon in Cancer this week is a new chapter on many levels. Indeed, you do have big changes occurring; significant happenings draw harmony, balance, and emotional fulfillment. It's a sense of expansion that offers freedom and growth. You touch down in an enterprising landscape that helps you develop goals. You become involved with a venture that takes flight and soars to dizzy heights. It does put the shine on your talents as it grows your abilities exponentially.

Communication arrives out of the left field. It is from someone who's been out of the loop for a few months. It does bring a catch up of gossip, and it puts you in the right frame of mind to keep connected with this person and others in your social circle. It brings a time of vibrant conversations that connect the dots on supportive and engaging communication. Being the focus of attention draws confidence and shines a light on a happy time.

Information arrives that shines a light on an online event. It does connect you with others in your community. It marks a bold beginning as you open a path that supports growth and learning. It lays the groundwork to communicate with a social environment. Improving your situation brings transformation to your door. It is indicative of the uptick of options ready to flow into your life. A flurry of possibilities soon emerges.

You link to an aspect that involves developing an intriguing enterprise. Something is in the pipeline; a positive trend sets the scene for new opportunities to emerge. Pacing yourself, prioritizing leads, and focusing on avenues of growth draws dividends. It does connect you with a path towards your dreams. It has you working on improving security and developing your skills in new areas. It offers a firm and robust basis from which to grow your career path.

It marks a time of building foundations grounded and able to restore equilibrium. It lets you take stock of where you hope to go next. Plotting a course forward brings the stepping-stones necessary to develop a tangible system towards your destination. Ideas gain traction, and you soon immerse yourself in working towards your vision. It brings a new strategy that let you work smarter and more efficiently.

Careful calculations discern the right path ahead. Carefully considering your options brings a practical approach that draws concrete results. Long-awaited news arrives soon, and this keeps your energy charged with inspiration. It connects you with a path that grows your potential. Home-grown opportunities await your innovative and enterprising touch. An idea bursts to life and begins a wildfire of inspiration that fans the flames of creativity.

FEBRUARY

Sun	Mon	Tue	Wed	Thu	Fri	Sat
		1	2	3	4	5
6	7	8	9	10	11	12
13	14	15	16	17	18	19
20	21	22	23	24	25	26
27	28					

ASTROLOGY

February 1st - New Moon in Aquarius 05:45
February 1st - Chinese New Year (Tiger)
February 1st - Imbolc

February 4th - Mercury Retrograde ends in Capricorn

February 8th - First Quarter Moon in Taurus 13:50

February 16th - Mercury at Greatest Western Elongation
February 16th - Snow Moon. Full Moon in Leo 16:57

February 23rd - Last Quarter Moon in Scorpio 22:32

NEW MOON

FULL MOON

27

FEBRUARY WEEK ONE

You reach a turning point that lets you slow down and discover pathways you may have missed in your rush to reach a destination. It does bring a focus on your home environment. Improving your circumstances is a priority. Grounding yourself in everyday routines bring stability into your world. It lets you plan resources and plot a course for growth. Exploring possibilities gets you ready to spread your wings and develop your vision.

New information brings a surge of confidence as it lets you explore a new possibility. Your intuition is your compass; it helps you reinvent your life with a new path forward. It brings a shift that takes you out of your comfort zone and challenges you to lean into learning a new area. It brings a chapter where you tackle research, growth, and the development of goals. It does light a passage towards improving your bottom line.

Mercury Retrograde ends in Capricorn, and it dials down stress and has you feeling inspired as the possibilities seem limitless. The more you improve your circumstances, the more life does line up options that shift your situation forward. Being open to new opportunities and experiences opens the gate to a brighter future. Considering your options carefully lets you choose wisely and effectively.

FEBRUARY WEEK TWO

There is an improvement coming around home and family life. It brings an excellent outlet for excess energy. It draws an essential time of advancing goals and developing an area worth your time. As you secure a strong foundation, you grow your world and set your sights on a lofty vision. It draws a productive landscape that eases stress and harnesses your creativity to advance your dreams. As you paint the backdrop to this canvas, you begin to fill the finer details of where this path leads.

It is a landmark time that brings new information on the winds of change. It reveals an area that spurs you on to action. Developing this journey becomes a big focus. It is a lucky break that lets you plot your course forward and step out in a new environment. As things come together, you see your life's passage in a new light. Even the challenges are worth their gold weight as they grow your spirit and teach otherwise inaccessible wisdom. Resilience and tenacity heighten; you take actions during this time that cracks the code to developing your life.

You are ready to head towards smoother waters. It does bring a carefree and happy time to let your guard down in a social setting. A change of scenery ahead brings a willingness to build your personal life openly. It brings inspiration flowing into your world. It removes stagnant and outworn areas and encourages the experimentation of new pathways.

FEBRUARY WEEK THREE

The Full Moon in Leo this week does wipe the slate clean on many levels. This time is a catalyst for change. It brings an opportunity that helps you break free of current limitations. It lets you unwrap a fantastic phase that brings you to a time of harmony. An emphasis on increasing stability brings a sterling chapter that blesses your life with new potential.

You accomplish a great deal by being flexible and staying open to new information. News arrives that propels you forward towards a course of action that grows your world. The pace and rhythm of life pick up as you chart a course towards advancing your abilities into new areas. An attractive avenue opens, and this generates excitement. It brings a dynamic phase of productivity and busyness.

News arrives that brings a new direction. Exploring options let you plot a course towards a new area. It releases challenges and guides you towards an inspiring path of growing your abilities. Life is ripe with potential, and expanding your reach into new regions draws fruitful results. It sets the stone for a broader journey that encompasses pathways of advancement. It puts the shine on your skills and helps you create a grounded environment.

FEBRUARY WEEK FOUR

Your career path ahead is to an upswing. Trying new options polishes your talents and advances your abilities into areas that grow your potential. You discover a new role is on offer. It brings responsibilities and involves learning a course that develops your abilities. It brings an extensive and progressive phase that helps you climb the ladder to success. You make the best choices possible for your career path, and this paves the way for advancement. Planning enables you to realize a dream position that makes the most of your skillset. It kickstarts an enriching and rewarding phase of developing your goals. You pour your energy into cultivating this opportunity and unearth a rewarding result. Information arrives that that gets your goals on track. It helps you create space to nurture your dreams. You plant the seeds that blossom into an active and productive phase of developing the path ahead. Seeing your life progress forward makes a big difference; it flings the window open on a sunny aspect that warms your spirit.

Opportunities to socialize tempt you towards expansion. It brings an adventurous road that lifts your spirits. Lively discussions set the scene for an active chapter of growth in your social life. Seeing things on the move clears the slate; it brings goals that soon become a priority in your world. Chasing success and happiness drives your vision forward. A river of hopes and dreams merge with a sea of understanding about where to head next.

MARCH

Sun	Mon	Tue	Wed	Thu	Fri	Sat
		1	2	3	4	5
6	7	8	9	10	11	12
13	14	15	16	17	18	19
20	21	22	23	24	25	26
27	28	29	30	31		

ASTROLOGY

March 2nd - New Moon in Pisces 17:34

March 10th - First Quarter Moon in Gemini 10:45

March 18th - Worm Moon. Full Moon in Virgo 07:17

March 20th - Ostara/Spring Equinox 15:33

March 25th - Last Quarter Moon in Capricorn 05:37

NEW MOON

FULL MOON

MARCH WEEK ONE

New Moon in Pisces reveals a new undercurrent of potential that surrounds your life. The surprise news ahead heightens creativity and offers a chance to learn a new area. It points you in the right direction to head to a breakthrough and reach a turning point that ushers in more settled energy. Limitations and blockages no longer hold you back from exploring new horizons. Cultivating your interests brings contact with like-minded people who support your journey of growth and revolution. Pieces of the puzzle fall into place, drawing abundance and happiness. Creating space to channel your excess energy touches you down in an area ripe for development.

You reveal an exciting avenue that lights a path towards building your dreams. Your intuition guides the journey forward as it sweeps in new adventures and more freedom. It does initiate a social vibe that brings a cast of characters into your world. A new companion shakes up your environment. This person brings an exciting contrast that adds a rainbow of colors into your world. Spending time with friends and companions heightens well-being as it replenishes depleted emotional tanks. It is a path that brings happiness and expansion into focus.

You reveal an enterprising option that gets the ball rolling on developing your career path. It does bring learning and growth. Your ability to navigate an expansive and somewhat complex phase lets you come out on top and enjoy a rewarding chapter that advances your capabilities. You discover that hurdles and obstacles are merely invitations to find workarounds and head towards growth. It takes a little while to achieve the next level; the effective changes ahead suggest you are on the right track to progressing your skills forward. You see results that are gratifying and tick the right boxes.

Information ahead brings attractive opportunities for creativity and self-expression. It highlights a path that offers ample room to grow your abilities. It brings collaborations with other artistic types. You forge a new friendship, and being with this person draws a stable and calming influence. It grounds your foundations in a productive chapter right for growth. You implement strategies that offer a passageway to a brighter future. It brings a dynamic and busy time of working with your abilities and putting the polish on your skills.?

You lift the lid on a curious option that brings a new possibility to your life. You reveal information that sparks a path of discovery. It helps you reach the dawn of a new area that gets a stable growth and expansion phase. It positively influences your life and enriches your environment.

MARCH WEEK THREE

A Full Moon in Virgo this week. At the end of the week, Ostara/Spring Equinox brings the Sun again after the long winter. A clue ahead expands your energy towards this turning point. It brings a social aspect that connects you with other trailblazers. Initiating a new endeavor sets the scene for a journey that inspires and delights. There is movement ahead for your social life that sparks with magic. You have a secret admirer who is currently keeping their feelings under wraps. They are looking for the right time to connect with you and get the ball rolling on developing conversations that deepen the potential. Sharing with this person encourages growth and expansion. It triggers a highly creative time of blending ideas and thoughts with another who has an artistic flair for life.

You uncover a journey that holds you in good stead and helps you reach a higher growth level. Your perseverance is admirable and does bring a chance to debut your talents to a broader audience. You land in a creative environment that sparks a journey worth your time. Pinpointing the correct rungs in the ladder lets you climb towards success efficiently and effectively. It brings a vivid and dynamic phase that grows your skills and advances your abilities to the next level.

MARCH WEEK FOUR

Your patience and perseverance reward you when you discover news that tempts you forward. It leads to ample time for enriching conversations and a bonus that lifts your spirits. Suppose you have found your motivation and energy flagging. In that case, this changes as you dive into a lively chapter that brings expansion to your social life. It is a positive turn of events that nurtures well-being and draws abundance into your surroundings.

Events conspire to crack the code on a wide-open road of potential. While change can feel disconcerting, it does open new possibilities that inspire growth. You reveal information that illuminates an area of interest. It gives you the chance to implement strategies that develop goals. It helps you launch forward towards an enterprising chapter. A creative aspect brings vital energy that reboots and rejuvenates your environment.

You benefit from events on the horizon as a new page opens in your book of life. It initiates a path that grows your skills and broadens your circle of friends. A prominent area comes calling, and this brings an exciting road of new adventures. It is a remarkable chance to grow your vision outwardly. It brings gifts and good luck that improves stability and grounds your foundations in an area worth progressing.

APRIL

Sun	Mon	Tue	Wed	Thu	Fri	Sat
					1	2
3	4	5	6	7	8	9
10	11	12	13	14	15	16
17	18	19	20	21	22	23
24	25	26	27	28	29	30

ASTROLOGY

April 1st - New Moon in Aries 06:24

April 9th - First Quarter Moon in Cancer 06:47

April 16th - Pink Moon. Full Moon in Libra 18:54

April 22nd - Lyrids Meteor Shower from April 16-25

April 23rd - Last Quarter Moon in Aquarius 11:56.

April 29th - Mercury Greatest Eastern Elongation of 20.6 degrees from the Sun.

April 30th - New Moon in Taurus 20:27

NEW MOON

FULL MOON

43

New Moon in Aries this week gives the green light to move forward towards developing an area of interest. A communitive element in the air brings news and information. It boosts your motivation and lets you share thoughts and ideas with others who support your dreams. It brings increasing stability on the home front. Something you have been hoping to achieve reaches fruition. It brings the right time to progress your vision forward.

Your social life holds an upward trend that offers room to develop and nurture a new bond. Drinking in this engaging environment quenches your thirst for adventure. Being with this individual is a welcome distraction; it improves your life on many levels. It does bring a bountiful chapter of moving forward with purposefulness. It's a journey that nurtures the creative magic that surrounds your world.

You are transitioning towards a life event that brings benefits. A new chapter emerges that blends with heightened creativity. You find the road suddenly clears and an expansive oasis of possibilities tempt you forward. Being open to change helps you build foundations that are stable and ripe for progression. Information arrives soon that orientates you to a new journey. You can clear the decks and prepare for a fresh start. The alchemy of manifestation is brewing in your world's background; it highlights a path of expansion.

The goodness and joy flow into your life when information reaches you, sparks a new chapter. It involves a time of fun and adventure. A lighter phase of social engagement tempts you forward. It does bring a chance to converse with friends, and this supports your well-being. You blaze through a time that is self-expressive, creative, and progressive. You discover that little stands in the way between being able to develop your dreams and aspirations. It does bring the motivation to explore new pathways of growth and expansion.

You open new possibilities that bring a transition to a happy chapter of developing goals. An undercurrent of exciting potential surrounds your life. It fires up inspiration and conveys the motivation necessary to expand your horizons into new areas. Getting involved with a passion project releases the pressure; it sparks renewal and healing. It provides you with ample room to grow your dreams. Innovative stirrings heighten creativity bringing steller ideas that help give voice to your true calling. It lets you tap into a little worn path towards advancement.

Information ahead brings a shift forward that is a source of inspiration. It's an important signpost that helps you plot a course towards achieving a long-held dream. You still have quite a journey in front of you, but it all begins with a single step towards your vision.

There is incoming potential likely to surge in your social life. A golden exchange with another develops into a collaboration that draws potential to light. It gives you a broader reach in which to spread your wings and take flight towards your vision. Beneficial changes ahead let you glimpse new options.

Some goals come to fruition, which clears the space for a fresh chapter to emerge. It lets you contemplate the path ahead with more freedom and creativity. It brings a time that enables you to embrace developing new options. It does offer a sideline to progress a business idea. Creating a strategic plan maps out innovative ideas and places you in the box seat to expand your horizons and achieve the right growth level. The past has been all about unearthing wisdom and growing your abilities. It has been challenging and taught you the value of resilience. The strength you carry is well worn and tinged with knowledge. You benefit from a lucky chapter that brings new ventures ahead. It lets you start fresh and broaden your horizons. It brings foundations that are perfect for a progressive phase of developing a lofty vision.

It places you in the right alignment to enjoy smooth sailing. If you have felt constrained by issues surrounding your situation, this will no longer cause conflict. Broadening your perception, you take in new areas of potential. A broad landscape awaits your willingness to explore possibilities.

APRIL WEEK FOUR

Lyrids Meteor Shower brings a powerhouse of fresh energy into your environment. A theme emerging relates to increasing opportunities ahead. You have weathered the storm and soon set sail towards smoother waters. Exploring new options, especially technology-related, brings a benefit to your world. It supports creativity, self-expression, and growth. A flexible and adaptable approach grounds your energy and stabilizes your foundations.

News shines a light on a chapter you can embrace as it captures the essence of magic. It takes time to unfurl the potential possible fully. It aligns you towards growing an avenue that offers dividends. It has you thinking about the future in an optimistic light.

Mercury Greatest Eastern Elongation can feel disquieting but curious news arrives that provides a side option. It brings a boost to morale as you see your situation improving by leaps and bounds. There is plenty of potential coming into your life that helps you move forward towards developing your goals. It enables you to plot a course towards an area that inspires your heart. It sets the tone for improving your personal life. It draws a happier chapter, a significant shift as you have been through some trials recently. It marks a path of abundance that brings security and serenity.

.

MAY

Sun	Mon	Tue	Wed	Thu	Fri	Sat
1	2	3	4	5	6	7
8	9	10	11	12	13	14
15	16	17	18	19	20	21
22	23	24	25	26	27	28
29	30	31				

ASTROLOGY

May 6th - Eta Aquarids Meteor Shower, April 19th - May 28th

May 9th - First Quarter Moon in Leo 00:21

May 10th - Mercury Retrograde begins in Gemini

May 16th - Total Lunar Eclipse 01:32

May 16th - Flower Moon. Full Moon in Scorpio 04:13

May 22nd - Last Quarter Moon in Aquarius 18:43

May 30th - New Moon in Leo 00:21

NEW MOON

FULL MOON

51

Eta Aquarids Meteor Shower brings an opportunity to broaden your vision; it brings a time of expansion, freedom, and optimism. You blaze through an uninterrupted time of progressing potential. It gets the magic coursing through your life and signifies a theme of improving your circumstances. It leaves you feeling optimistic about the potential possible. Implementing a smart strategy lets you avoid common pitfalls that could derail your progress. Putting your thinking cap on creates a plan that is robust and tinged with gold.

Life enters a new chapter when an alliance emerges. A meaningful situation is coming that puts the spotlight on a refreshing companion. Indeed, this person brings a curious element into your world. It focuses on drawing harmony, which sees a boost that restores inspiration and energy. Lively discussions set the chapter for a bountiful phase of connection and companionship. It does have you thinking outside of the box.

An opportunity arrives that positively resonates potential. It does spark your interest and rules the type of advancement that lets you build security. Getting involved with this venture supports your dreams. Things are on the move, and as your focus shifts forward, you discover an option that seems too good to be true. It is a path that holds water, and it brings an active and bustling phase of developing and growing this option.

MAY WEEK TWO

Mercury retrograde causes mayhem and disruption in your social life when it begins in Gemini this week. You find that setting barriers with people who are disingenuous and self-motivated helps ease the discord. Removing the drama alleviates stress and tension, and it has you feeling more hopeful about future possibilities. Indeed, you are undergoing a transition that culminates in a new chapter. It helps you navigate complex environments and come out a winner.

Taking personal inventory is imperative to discerning the direction ahead. Without going over the nuts and bolts of your life, you are flying blind, and this can lead to feeling directionless. Taking stock with a fair and impartial outlook lets you discover areas that would otherwise fly under the radar. It encourages expansion through your willingness to sift and sort ideas until you refine and blend your vision into a rare and precious gemstone.

There is an emphasis on improving home life that offers hope for a brighter future. The rough edges smooth over, bringing a remarkable chance to develop a happier and more harmonious environment. Good fortune flows into your world and finds its level. It stabilizes foundations and lets you ease troubles, and make headway towards developing your vision.

MAY WEEK THREE

Flower Moon. The Full Moon in Scorpio brings new possibilities to contemplate after what has been an unsettling time. Tapping into this potential lets, you get a creative project off the ground. It helps you launch into the next active phase of growth and progression. It puts the shine on talents and lets you add a dash of sunshine to your world. You open a clear path that tempts you to focus your energy on a meaningful area. Creating outlets such as this improves the foundations in your world.

Substance and joy flow into your world, bringing goals you can develop. Opportunity comes knocking; this sees potential blossoming and does bring creative options worth growing. You plant the seeds that blossom into a significant journey forward. It takes you towards a more social time that connects you with kindred spirits. Setting intentions create the right mindset to push back barriers and step forward into your next life phase.

A friend seeks to become closer, which opens a door as it brings a bond that leaves you feeling inspired. Opportunities to collaborate with this person gets a sense of kinship. It takes you towards a productive environment that helps you expand your horizons in new directions. A new destination is coming, which sees life picking up the pace. It lands you in an ideal position to progress your goals.

MAY WEEK FOUR

A New Moon in Leo sees information arrives that clears the clouds away. Sonny skies breeze into your life as it opens a path forward. It alleviates stress and tensions and fuels inspiration. The floodgates of potential are opening, giving you a chance to use your talents and grow your abilities. It's a positive sign that advancement is looming. A big decision is coming up, and it sparks with possibility. It is a time that offers a fascinating and curious track towards growth.

An outstanding opportunity arrives and brings a chance to develop a new enterprise. Your creativity is running high and carving out time to spend developing this project draws well-being. It puts delays behind you and lets you plan ambitiously for future growth. It renews your spirit and blesses your energy with inspiration. It brings a time of joyful possibilities that put you in an expansive and optimistic mood. You've had your share of trials and can enjoy the smoother passage through to a more harmonious phase. You have been going through a transition, and this news connects you to a path worth growing. You get word of an offer soon that sweeps in exciting potential. It helps you sail through a progressive time that lets you develop an area of interest. A sense of wanderlust is driving back barriers and encouraging expansion. It is a time of increasing self-expression and creativity that helps you discover new ambitions. Well crafted ideas are ready to be fine-tuned and built into tangible results.

JUNE

Sun	Mon	Tue	Wed	Thu	Fri	Sat
			1	2	3	4
5	6	7	8	9	10	11
12	13	14	15	16	17	18
19	20	21	22	23	24	25
26	27	28	29	30		

ASTROLOGY

June 3rd - Mercury Retrograde ends in Taurus

June 7th - First Quarter Moon in Virgo 14:48

June 14th - Strawberry Moon. Full Moon in Sagittarius Supermoon 11:51

June 16th - Mercury's greatest Western elongation of 23.2 degrees from the Sun

June 21st - Last Quarter Moon in Aries 03:11

June 21st - Midsummer/Litha Solstice 09:13

June 29th - New Moon in Cancer 02:52

NEW MOON

FULL MOON

Mercury Retrograde ends in Taurus. You head towards a chapter that glimmers with potential. It rebuilds your world as an opportunity comes knocking that tempts you to expand your comfort zone. It launches you towards progressing in a meaningful situation. Taking time to nurture this environment increases the potential possible. It brings significant change and helps you achieve a fantastic outcome. You soon tap into a path of promise. It does lead to an approach that highlights emerging abundance as it lets you get in touch with your inner guidance system. Listening to your intuition shines a light on the direction ahead. You start exploring areas that hold meaning.

Your efforts are recognized soon. It brings a rewarding time that offers progression. Taking the initiative helps you achieve the highest result. It does get an active time of moving life forward with a strong emphasis on growth. Adding new items to your schedule heightens potential and brings a unique opportunity to light. It does grow your abilities and broaden your trajectory.

You turn a corner and shine in an expressive and creative environment. It does connect you with a social phase that brings new people into your world. Surprise communication lifts the lid on a fresh chapter for your personal life. It is a continuation of a more comprehensive theme of expanding horizons occurring in your social life.

JUNE WEEK TWO

The Full Moon in Sagittarius Supermoon at week's end brings a curious benefit. Information arrives soon, which is highly motivating. It lets you flex your abilities in a new direction. It offers a real and valid chance to progress your talents. Being proactive draws dividends. Improvements are on the horizon that let you test the waters before jumping into the deep end. Exploring higher levels advances your abilities and grows your talents.

You power through towards a productive chapter. Impressive results breathe life into your dreams, and this takes your vision further. Clearing blocks and establishing stable foundations lights a path of growth in your career sector. Favorable information advances your skills. The seeds you plant blossom into moving your abilities into new areas. It helps you maneuver forward and navigate a complex environment. As prospects heighten, streamlining and rearranging goals becomes imperative. Your awareness shifts, and this encourages expansion.

Some beautiful changes are looming. You enter an ambitious and energizing time that helps you create progress. It brings new possibilities that inspire and motivate. It enables you to release outworn areas that didn't reach fruition. Streamlining and refining the path ahead draws a new flow of possibilities. It brings growth into your life, and forward motion propels you towards an enterprising chapter.

JUNE WEEK THREE

Midsummer/Litha Solstice at week's end is an ideal time to reflect on your goals. While things may be currently slow, new opportunities are still available if you take the time to explore new pathways. A creative undertaking you become involved with soon takes shape and begins to branch out into different areas. It brings liberation, freedom, and expansion. It reinvigorates optimism, drive, and purpose. The pace of life becomes active and dynamic ahead.

There is plenty of excitement ahead when someone reaches out, which leaves you feeling excited about the possibilities. The journey begins in a fledgling stage; a great deal is possible as things move forward with this person. Soon enough, open discussions create fertile ground for ideas to blossom. It brings a sense of connection into focus; you feel hopeful about this individual's future possibilities.

Changes ahead draw new possibilities to your personal life. It brings a winning chapter that lets you deepen a bond with a charming character. You receive gentle support to expand horizons and develop an area of interest. It draws engaging conversations with someone who offers support, guidance, and wisdom. Blending ideas with another heightens creative expression and leads to a golden phase.

JUNE WEEK FOUR

The New Moon in Cancer shows that the future is looking brighter all the time. A new chapter ahead brings stable foundations for your life. It creates space to nurture bonds, and this releases doubt and worry. It draws supportive energy, and life blooms with new potential. Life becomes a blaze of activity and opportunity. The power of magic surrounds your social life. Your willingness to expand horizons draws an enriching phase. It lets you weed out situations that failed to reach fruition; this removes the drama and focuses on what truly counts. Stimulating conversations brings an energizing chapter ahead.

You can look forward to a refreshing change of pace. It brings a time that is forthright, empowering, and ambitious. It does draw opportunities that hold promise. Investing in developing your abilities lets you obtain the highest result possible. It brings a gateway of growth that expands your knowledge base. It does help you establish yourself in an area that grows your talents. It is a potent time for higher learning and self-development. The options ahead tug on your awareness.

An opportunity is coming that opens the gateway to an active environment. It lets you revolutionize life from the ground up. Heightened security brings robust foundations. Lighter energy flows into your life and lines you up with an original path worth growing. It places you in the box seat to take your talents to the next level.

JULY

Sun	Mon	Tue	Wed	Thu	Fri	Sat
					1	2
3	4	5	6	7	8	9
10	11	12	13	14	15	16
17	18	19	20	21	22	23
24	25	26	27	28	29	30
31						

ASTROLOGY

July 7th - First Quarter Moon in Libra 02:14

July 13th - Buck Moon. Full Moon in Capricorn. Supermoon 18:37

July 20th - Last Quarter Moon in Aries 14:18

July 28th - New Moon in Leo 17:54

July 28th - Delta Aquarids Meteor Shower. July 12th - August 23rd

NEW MOON

FULL MOON

67

JULY WEEK ONE

Attractive options get you thinking about the possibilities. Inspiration burns brightly, and this lets you strike gold as you turn the corner on a winning chapter. It enables you to carve out time to expand horizons and bring new possibilities to life. You are given a leg up to an environment that draws balance. It lets you slow down and explore pathways of growth. Being open to change underscores a willingness to unearth new possibilities. It brings information to your table that has you thinking about the path ahead in a new light. You discover enterprising activities that advance your abilities. As your prospects heighten, it brings new terrain to explore. It activates a phase of pushing back barriers and nurturing new adventures. Opportunity comes knocking, and it brings a new chapter of golden potential to your door.

A golden aspect weaves its way through your life. It brings a remarkable shift that helps you pursue goals and creative enterprises on the home front. It lets you create space to build your foundations from the ground up. A situation you invest your energy into soon blossoms into a meaningful journey that inspires your heart. Indeed, exploring new avenues of growth breaks up stagnant energy patterns. Pushing the boundaries back liberates restrictions and sees you head towards new adventures. It is exhilarating and enriching. In particular, one person seeks to become closer, and this companion inspires a great deal of personal growth.

JULY WEEK TWO

The Full Moon in Capricorn is the second Supermoon for this year. You've dealt with challenges and can now reap the benefits. Fortifying foundations draw stability; a vital transition takes you towards a more productive and active landscape. It begins with a bustling phase of growing goals and developing your dreams. There is a strong focus on home life and advancing your abilities into new areas. Abundant life options ahead draw stability and improve the building blocks.

Life is getting over a hump but will soon become busier. An enterprising offer lands at your feet, and this has you thinking about the possibilities. It brings an opportunity in your local community that connects you with people and characters that light up new potential across the board. It helps create the stepping stones necessary to expand your social life. It brings a stimulating environment that draws lively discussions and the sharing of thoughts and ideas. As you head towards this productive chapter, you can appreciate how far you have come on your journey.

There is a focus on developing your social life ahead. Expanding options bring harmony into focus. It does offer a chance to connect with others in your community. It draws a smoother ride and a more abundant landscape. Utilizing technology to your advantage lets you communicate with a crew of lively characters. It sets the tone for developing friendships and developing foundations.

JULY WEEK THREE

Communication ahead brings excitement. It offers a chance to nurture a closer friendship, and this provides a promising path forward. Feeling the sense of connection brings a social aspect into focus as life sparkles with refreshing potential. It brings changes that emphasize improvement on the home front. If you have felt moorings, have been adrift recently, connecting with this supporter draws stability. It lets you nurture an area of interest, and this shines a light on harmony and well-being.

Things heat up when you discover a deeper bond with someone who seeks to join your inner circle. It brings a fruitful time of thoughtful conversations as you ride a wave of hopeful energy with this person. Discovering a more connected and supportive bond is possible takes you towards a groundbreaking phase of potential. Trusting your intuition helps guide a foundation from which to grow your social life.

A time of abundance and magic is looming. It marks a turning point as you discover a closer bond is possible with an individual who brings a touch of magic into your life. A buzz of social activity gets a chance to share dialogues and discussions with someone you find intriguing. It does kick off a productive chapter for your personal life. Spending time with this person brings the sharing of thoughts and ideas that nurture your spirit.

New Moon in Leo and the Delta Aquarids Meteor Shower nurture creativity. You are ready for a new chapter. Luck is on your side as a path emerges soon that opens the door to a new possibility. It does bring change an opportunity to grow your talents. It brings a cycle that sets in motion new options. Life moves from strength to strength; your willingness to navigate hurdles lets you come out on top of things. A new project brings excitement as the fires of inspiration burn brightly around this venture. It does get a chance to focus on tasks and endeavors that sparks your interest.

Things are on the move for you soon. It draws a time that sets your life ablaze with new potential. You chart a course towards developing a goal, and this has the potential to deliver excellent results. Your willingness to stay open to change draws a valuable reward. It revolves around learning a new area, and this creates a productive phase of growth. It has you focusing on developing dreams and traversing a progressive path. A bustling phase of expansion draws well-being as life becomes busy and you get on with the hustle of nailing your vision.

The tides turn in your favor soon. It lets you unpack a rich environment worth your time and effort. Opening a pathway towards growth sets the stage for an impressive time of advancing goals. It supports learning and development and lets you focus on an area that nurtures skills and talents.

AUGUST

Sun	Mon	Tue	Wed	Thu	Fri	Sat
	1	2	3	4	5	6
7	8	9	10	11	12	13
14	15	16	17	18	19	20
21	22	23	24	25	26	27
28	29	30	31			

ASTROLOGY

August 5th - First Quarter Moon Scorpio 11:06

August 8th - Full Moon in Aquarius Supermoon 01:35. Sturgeon Moon.

August 8th - Perseids Meteor Shower July 17th - August 24th

August 14th - Saturn at Opposition

August 19th - Last Quarter Moon in Taurus 04:36

August 27th - New Moon in Virgo 08:16

August 27th - Mercury at Greatest Eastern Elongation at 27.3 degrees from the Sun

NEW MOON

FULL MOON

75

AUGUST WEEK ONE

You reveal information soon that opens a gateway towards a fresh start. An opportunity ahead brings a gift of stability. It brings a breakthrough that offers a turning point for your goals. You take in a cycle of prosperity that is currently on the periphery of your environment. Broadening the scope of your perception brings a fruitful time of nurturing talents and expanding horizons. It brings fundamental changes that encourage renewal. It speaks of news that is a catalyst for change. A vital clue arrives that brings a possibility to the surface. It is a unique opportunity that offers growth and learning. Advancing your skills into a new area begins an upward trend that provides room to progress your talents and abilities. It does have you feeling on track and excited about future potential. It connects you with others who are on a similar path. It brings the spirit of adventure into focus as you merge with kindred souls to discuss ideas and plan future goals.

An emphasis on fun and friendship ahead draws lightness and levity into your world. Good news arrives out of the blue and takes you by surprise. It links you up with kindred spirits and brings the chance to expand your social circle. It brings replenishment to your emotional tank. Stabilizing foundations brings a robust climate as past struggles fade away. You open a new page on your book of life, bringing the energy of inspiration, motivation, and joy flowing into your environment.

AUGUST WEEK TWO

Full Moon in Aquarius Supermoon and the Perseids Meteor Shower this week sees a note arrives that empowers you to expand your horizons. It brings an emphasis on improving your social life and does draw lightness and abundance into your world. You feel a positive influence beneath your wings as you navigate the path ahead adeptly. Past troubles fade away as you get involved with expanding options. It brings perfect conditions to plot a course towards a new enterprise. It helps you create sustainable change and release the stress and tension. It gives you the green light to chase your dreams and grow your circumstances. A full chapter ahead elevates prospects. It brings a chance to grow and learn in a new area. It gets a bonus that adds luck and inspiration. Gathering wisdom, plotting the course ahead lets you weave a basket of success.

It speaks of a diverse path that brings unique people into your world. Your ability to nurture bonds forges the right type of connections. It does lay the groundwork for expansion in your social life. Being true to yourself cracks open the gateway to developing your world. It brings a sense of support and connection that hits the sweet spot. You discover people who hold similar interests and ideals.

AUGUST WEEK THREE

The path ahead opens as you make adjustments and streamline priorities to bring the best to the top. An exciting element in the air has you seeking a solution for your restlessness. It takes you on a journey of new horizons that sparks movement and discovery. It lets you grow and expand your social life. It takes you towards a happy chapter of connecting with kindred spirits. Increasing your inner circle brings the right tone for your life.

You are ready to open the curtains and embrace sunshine ahead. It brings a time that resonates warmly with enriching experiences. It lets you take a break and do something just for yourself. It marks the beginning of a journey that is inspired and adventurous. Following this path of certainty sees your inspiration flourishing under sunny skies. It places you in the starting box to grow your vision.

Information arrives that cracks the code to the chapter ahead. It does bring a chance to study, learn, and grow your talents. Being open to new options lets you transition forward and build a foundation based on your current goals and desires. It creates a stable platform to expand your world. As you amplify your success rate, new opportunities continue to flow, revolutionizing the potential possible.

In Virgo this week, New Moon combined with Mercury at Greatest Eastern Elongation from the Sun to heighten potential. A slow but steady transformation improves your world. Life holds a glittering possibility; it connects you with someone who inspires, and this brings happiness. You plot a course towards developing your life. Events unfold and bring an enriching chapter to light. Emotional well-being soars, and confidence is on the rise as you share insightful discussions with someone attentive and thoughtful.

New people emerge in your social life, and improvement is at the crux of the changes ahead. Life becomes a curious blend of exploring new possibilities for your social life. It does refuel your emotional tank and connects you with a person who sparks your interest. Staying open to new opportunities and people feeds your creativity; it inspires growth and motivates change. Excitement and adventure bring a journey worth growing.

Clear skies breeze into your life as something special arrives for you soon. Your fortune changes for the better; it lets you embark on a path of expansion. A pivotal moment ahead brings a new possibility to life. It releases stress and tension; it enables you to take the first step towards developing a journey that inspires your heart. You can wipe the slate clean and remove outworn aspects as this new pathway emerges.

.

SEPTEMBER

Sun	Mon	Tue	Wed	Thu	Fri	Sat
				1	2	3
4	5	6	7	8	9	10
11	12	13	14	15	16	17
18	19	20	21	22	23	24
25	26	27	28	29	30	

ASTROLOGY

September 7th - First Quarter Moon Sagittarius 18:08

September 10th - Mercury Retrograde begins in Libra

September 10th - Corn Moon. Harvest Moon. Full Moon in Pisces 09:58

September 16th - Neptune at Opposition

September 17th - Last Quarter Moon in Gemini 21:52

September 23 - Mabon/Fall Equinox. 01:03

September 25th - New Moon in Libra 21:54

September 26th - Jupiter at Opposition

NEW MOON

FULL MOON

You can create a wellspring of possibility by keeping an open mindset. Focusing on your vision and mapping out plans does let you gain a better sense of the direction ahead. There is an emphasis on improving your life. A significant influence flows into your world, soon bringing options that encourage growth and advancement. It has you moving towards an enterprising chapter.

It's a beautiful time to create space to nurture your goals. It does help you make progress and head towards an enterprising chapter. You discover a lead that brings a decision, enabling you to cut away from the drama. It places you in a strong position to achieve growth and nail your vision. A clean sweep of new possibilities blows into your life to tempt you forward.

Essential information is coming, and it brings curious news. It lets you turn a corner and head towards growth. Examining your motivation refines the potential. It enables you to strip away from areas that hinder progress. Nurturing this potential lets it blossom into an active and expansive chapter of growth and progress. It brings stable foundations that help you move beyond the barriers as you reveal an enriching landscape. A changing scene on the horizon leaves you feeling inspired. You are ready to make tracks on achieving your vision; growth is possible as you tend to this option.

Mercury Retrograde begins in Libra. Harvest Moon. Full Moon in Pisces The more you work on improving your circumstances, the more you can revel in smooth sailing. You see the past and the issues that hindered your progress. Restoring equilibrium creates space; it gives you a deep emotional awareness that brings healing and nourishment to your soul. Doing inner soul work may change your priorities, so keep flexible and adaptable. Opening your mind to new possibilities and experiences advance your vision. It lets you spot the potential in an opportunity that crosses your path. It brings a breakthrough that opens the gate towards a brighter future.

A transition forward brings a new chapter. It holds a valuable breakthrough. The challenges you currently face are guiding you to explore new options. Your patience and perseverance bring a journey that draws harmony and brings joy into your life. It does see you hitting your groove when an offer lands in your lap. It restores faith in the path ahead. It is a time of reflection and contemplation. You may feel pulled back to the past, and this is to resolve and settle emotions. If you have found yourself feeling unsettled this month, it is a chance to create space to clear the path ahead. News of a new role arrives soon that underscores the abundance waiting on the periphery of your life. It sets the tone for a broader journey forward.

It is a time of change that sweeps away hostile areas. You can release all that stands in the way of your happiness. The universe supports growth and expansion. You are ready to remove the limitations and seek adventure. You discover fortune favors bold moves. A social environment comes into view that connects you with other like-minded individuals. It brings a busy time that opens the way forward. Your choices and decisions shape destiny as you merge with a kindred spirit.

You soon enter uncharted territory as new options arrive. It lets you plot a course towards a more social environment. It brings expansion that is exciting and tinged with gold. Your willingness to be open to new people and experiences sees life becoming happier and more expressive. It draws balance and rejuvenates your energy from the ground up. Communication arrives that brings a boost as it involves an invitation.

You soon begin exploring new possibilities; a positive trend ahead helps you develop reasonable solutions. It brings a path of expansion that draws new companions and areas of learning. Developing your talents brings a new flow of energy that encourages abundance. Creativity heightens as new possibilities a spark to life. Lightness and harmony flow into your world, bringing a boost to your social life. There is a change in your environment that removes the drama and leaves behind issues that prevented progress. Expanding your social circle creates an interconnected vine of support.

Mabon/Fall Equinox. New Moon in Libra. Jupiter at Opposition. There is a lot of raw potential surrounding your life, ready to be worked. It does connect you with others in your tribe who have similar goals in mind. Being receptive to new opportunities lets you take advantage of options that bring growth and learning into focus. It reveals a purposeful and innovative journey towards refining your talents. An idea takes off, and this begins a journey towards growing your foundations in new areas. The wind is beneath your wings, and you are unstoppable as you transition forward towards an enterprising phase of growth.

It speaks of opportunities ahead to develop your talents. Growing and expanding your skills opens pathways to dabble in an interest that inspires your mind. You get involved in an area that requires dedication and concentration. It does offer an entrepreneurial aspect and helps you find your niche in an environment rich with potential. You become involved in a venture that takes on a curious light. It brings the possibility of a partnership with another person. It brings a unique journey that ripples with gold. It's highly creative and resonates with movement and discovery.

New potential ahead brings possibilities to light. It seems a thoughtful gesture from another person touches your heart. It points you towards developing a bond that nurtures your life on many levels.

OCTOBER

Sun	Mon	Tue	Wed	Thu	Fri	Sat
						1
2	3	4	5	6	7	8
9	10	11	12	13	14	15
16	17	18	19	20	21	22
23	24	25	26	27	28	29
30	31					

ASTROLOGY

October 2nd - Mercury Retrograde ends in Virgo

October 3rd - First Quarter Moon in Capricorn 00.14

October 7th - Draconids Meteor Shower. Oct 6th -10th

October 8th - Mercury Greatest Western Elongation

October 9th - Hunters Moon. Full Moon in Aries 20:54

October 17th - Last Quarter Moon in Cancer 17.15

October 21st -Orionids Meteor Shower. October 2nd - November 7th

October 25th - New Moon in Scorpio 10:48

October 25th - Partial Solar Eclipse

NEW MOON

FULL MOON

Mercury Retrograde ends in Virgo. Feeling stuck or unsettled is a restless vibe that may impact you at this delicate juncture. You are transitioning forward, and this brings the room to grow your life. You soon set off on a new adventure that inspires your mind. Listening to the creativity within your spirit nurtures your talents and lights the way forward. It brings a social environment into focus, and this draws abundance.

It brings sunny skies to your personal life. It speaks of new beginnings and fresh starts that draw rejuvenation and healing into your world. Your willingness to open to new people and environments hold you in good stead. A focus on freedom and expansion connects you to a more social setting. It lets you turn a corner and shut the door on an area that feels done. Introductions at a social event get the ball rolling. You soon transition to a cycle that helps you solidify your goals and achieve a successful outcome. You receive word of an opportunity that doesn't come along every day. It inspires change; it brings a sense of synchronicity, which lets you know that it is the right choice for your life. It brings a social aspect that has you sharing interests with kindred spirits. You craft an experience that aligns with your passions.

You touch down on an exciting path when news reaches you about an unusual opportunity. Taking a little worn path offers new experiences and opportunities to grow. It does break out creativity and blaze a trail towards an active chapter.

OCTOBER WEEK TWO

A Full Moon in Aries lets you sink your teeth into an enterprising chapter. Changes in the air, fortune aligns to form a clear window to expand your trajectory. It brings an ambitious element that drives a growth-driven phase. You pour your energy into the path ahead, and it glimmers with potential. It lets you create a shift forward that takes you on a way of purpose and productivity. Progression is surprisingly swift and brings advancement.

It speaks of changes ahead that draw an influx of potential. It brings a beautiful time to nurture abilities and advance into a phase of expansion. It does get a choice, and a decision opens the gate towards developing an area of interest. It lets you find your feet after what has been a destabilizing chapter. Channeling your energy into a place that grows your life cleans the slate for a fresh chapter to emerge.

News ahead brings change; it does become a building block to a journey that offers room to improve stability. It highlights a path of imagination, creativity, and success. You have weathered a storm of choppy seas and can now embrace channeling your energy into an area of inspiration. A flood of potential creates a surge that carries you forward towards smoother waters. It brings a purposeful and innovative aspect. It introduces you to people and environments that are enriching. You unearth long-forgotten talents and begin to shine as you explore new pathways. It brings social outings and adventures.

OCTOBER WEEK THREE

It is a pivotal time that opens pathways of creativity and self-expression. It brings opportunities to grow skills and abilities. As confidence heightens, you become more proactive about expanding your life into new areas. Several cross-currents are flowing through your life's situation, which leads to confusion. Removing the deadwood lets, you see the trees in the forest of ideas. It unlocks clarity and clears the path ahead.

A gateway opens ahead that brings a journey of self-development and adventure. It triggers a path of new possibilities that draws rejuvenation. You discover potential around the corner that shines a light on advancing your vision. Allowing this opportunity to unfurl gently brings stable foundations. It helps you map out new goals and discover an exciting destination. It teams you up with a crew of kindred spirits.

It has been an unsettling time. Rapid change may leave you feeling drained and frazzled. Pausing to reflect and absorb troublesome vibrations draws healing and acceptance around buried areas. A positive influence comes into your life that illustrates the potential ready to bloom. It offers a path that highlights growth and progression. Discovering a new journey recalibrates your emotional slate. It brings improvement that provides an incredibly uplifting aspect. It wipes the slate clean as it releases emotional blocks that have been anchored in anxiety—freeing the stress grounds you in an environment that is stable and secure.

OCTOBER WEEK FOUR

New Moon in Scorpio with a Partial Solar Eclipse suggests that a path of higher wisdom and learning may call your name soon. It brings opportunities for self-development and personal growth. It brings the type of progress that enables you to chase a dream. Keeping an eye out for new leads lets you expand your horizons into a path worth growing. Spending time on beneficial activities draw wellness and abundance into your surroundings.

You may feel in the eye of the storm, but there is potential on the periphery of your vision that makes itself known soon. It helps you navigate a complicated time and branch out into a new area. A shift occurs that draws fundamental change; it sees you drifting away from outworn areas and embracing new possibilities. Choices and decisions ahead trigger a path of growth and learning. Planting your dreams in fertile soil sees them blossom into a successful journey forward. It brings the energy of abundance on the wind of change.

There is news on the horizon that brings insight into the path ahead. It begins a hero's journey of new adventures. It kickstarts growth as information is imminent that clears the way forward. It lets you create actual progress instead of being lost in fanciful dreaming. It brings a positive trend that sets the scene for progress and success. A new approach brings an innovative solution that lets you put the finishing touch on this time.

NOVEMBER

Sun	Mon	Tue	Wed	Thu	Fri	Sat
		1	2	3	4	5
6	7	8	9	10	11	12
13	14	15	16	17	18	19
20	21	22	23	24	25	26
27	28	29	30			

ASTROLOGY

November 1st - First Quarter Moon in Aquarius 06.37

November 4th - Taurids Meteor Shower. September 7th - December 10th

November 8th - Full Moon in Taurus 11:01 Beaver Moon. November 8th - Total Lunar Eclipse

November 9th - Uranus at Opposition

November 16th - Last Quarter Moon in Leo 13:27

November 17th - Leonids Meteor Shower Nov 6th-30th

November 23rd - New Moon in Sagittarius 22:57

November 30th - First Quarter Moon Pisces 14:36

NEW MOON

FULL MOON

NOVEMBER WEEK ONE

Taurids Meteor Shower sees life heads to an upswing when you discover opportunities that improve your world's security. It does draw a time that offers blessings as you land in a settled and grounded environment. It provides a gateway to developing new options. It illustrates a lighter approach that sees you head towards growth. Creative possibilities spark a social aspect that connects you with trailblazers and innovative types. A curious message arrives soon. Something is in the pipeline that becomes a big focus over the coming weeks. Your life is ripe with potential ready to blossom. It translates to a chapter that renews your energy, and it brings social options that are refreshing. Mingling with friends sets the tone for a happy time. It creates space to pause and reflect on the changes that swirl around your life. Exploring your options sweeps in the potential that jumpstarts the path forward. It's a time of growth and productivity. It reveals information that lets you reach your goals.

The future is looking rosy. It brings inspiring conversations and a fanciful aspect that has you wanting to expand your social life. It brings goals and aspirations to light that encourages you to open your life to new experiences. It heightens your confidence and marks a time of information and communication that light the path forward. If you feel at odds with your current trajectory, it gives you a chance to reboot and see the course ahead in a new light. You mark a significant turning point that offers room to grow your dreams.

Full Moon in Taurus with a Total Lunar Eclipse offers a rare gift. Your soul-searching draws clarity; it does bring insight into the path ahead. More extensive changes swirl around your life, and it can be not easy to know which direction to take next. You discover an essential clue soon that brings a new approach. It does offer expansion as a piece of the puzzle slips into place. Creating a solid base, you sweep aside outworn energy and embrace a sense of renewal that draws improvement.

The tides are turning in your favor. New potential on the horizon brings a busy time that offers an end to disappointment. It provides fresh inspiration and adventures that let you feel a lighter step as you walk out on the town. Confidence is on the rise, which sparks a journey that has you feeling optimistic about prospects. It builds a grounded foundation is that nurtures expansion in your social life.

You enter a time of expansion that improves the building blocks of stability in your personal life. It does align thoughts with sharing plans for growth with another. It reveals a journey right for development, and this sets the tone for an enterprising chapter of developing goals. Paying attention to the home front improves the foundations. Life picks up steam, and this brings an active phase ahead with someone who inspires your heart.

Leonids Meteor Shower sees life comes full circle when you hear from someone. This person touches base to see how you are as they have been thinking about you a great deal this year. It brings a new possibility into focus and begins a journey that develops a closer bond with someone you hold in high regard. It drives a chapter that offers fresh energy, which opens the path forward towards an abundant landscape.

The tides turn in your favor as you enter a bountiful time of increased potential around the home, social, and family life. It brings vital energy that has you exploring social opportunities with a gust of enterprising thoughtfulness. Mingling and networking bolster your confidence; it cracks open a path of abundance, kinship, and connection. Life offers you a chance to follow your passion and embrace a relationship with someone who inspires your mind. It is a path that blesses your life on many levels. It brings a chance to socialize in a community environment. As you attract positive outcomes, the essence of manifestation stirs up a new flow of enticing possibilities. It does have you dreaming about the future in a new way.

There is a focus on security and establishing grounded foundations. An area ripe with potential illuminates a social aspect. Stimulating conversations and lively discussions bring an active and dynamic social environment.

NOVEMBER WEEK FOUR

New Moon in Sagittarius You enter an energizing time that hits a high note. It opens a path that reveals new information. It governs a journey of progression, self-expression, creativity, and freedom. You craft the way ahead in alignment with a long-term vision. It triggers a chapter that draws security and blessings into your working life.

Good news arrives with a flurry of excitement that underscores the energy of magic and abundance. It creates a joyful shift forward that allows you to break free of limitations and focus on developing an area of interest. With this wind beneath your wings, you are unstoppable. It dials up creativity as you score an enticing new option. Life bustles with new energy, and the pace is progressive. It sparks change that brings a productive cycle that is both social and expansive.

Information currently percolating in the background of your social life soon makes an entrance. It creates an exciting mix of potential that offers a chance to plan ideas and share thoughts with someone who inspires your mind. It draws a bountiful time that provides support, guidance, and insight. You click well with this individual, and communication flows freely during brainstorming sessions. It takes you towards a chapter that is brighter, lighter, and in tune with your core beliefs. It nurtures your inspiration and fuels your spirit with good intentions.

DECEMBER

Sun	Mon	Tue	Wed	Thu	Fri	Sat
				1	2	3
4	5	6	7	8	9	10
11	12	13	14	15	16	17
18	19	20	21	22	23	24
25	26	27	28	29	30	31

ASTROLOGY

December 8th - Cold Moon. Moon Before Yule
December 8th - Full Moon in Gemini 04:07
December 8th - Mars at Opposition

December 13th - Geminids Meteor Shower. Dec 7th- 17th

December 16th - Last Quarter Moon in Virgo 08:56

December 21st - Ursids Meteor Shower December 17 - 25th December 21 - Mercury at Greatest Eastern elongation.
December 21st - Yule/Winter Solstice at 09:48

December 23rd - New Moon in Capricorn 10:16

December 29th - Mercury Retrograde begins in Capricorn

December 30th - First Quarter Moon Aries 01:21

NEW MOON

FULL MOON

You've been through an unpredictable time recently, but there is exciting potential brewing in your life's background. It makes itself known soon and clears the slate for a fresh chapter. Information arrives that shakes up the potential. It invigorates your spirit and offers an opportunity for growth. Incorporating this news into your plans is a pivotal moment. It unleashes your talents in an area ripe for progression. Exploring leads soon lets you head towards a direction that draws stable foundations. It allows you to reach for something more, and you soon enter an extended time of developing goals.

News arrives that helps you stay on top of the game in your working life. Many changes are surrounding your industry, and exploring new technologies, places you in the right alignment to capitalize on your talents. You benefit from a flexible and pragmatic approach as you prepare to embark on a new journey forward. Carefully exploring options lets, you obtain due diligence before embarking on your next chapter of growth.

A dear friend returns in your life, and this kicks off a chapter of sharing treasured memories. It does bring changes that stabilize foundations. It sees you improving your living situation. This person is smart and insightful; they open doors and bring generosity and wisdom to the table. It draws advancement into your home life and triggers an active phase of developing a bond that sparks potential.

Full Moon in Gemini. Mars at Opposition. Something on offer soon hits the sweet spot. It reveals a path of movement and discovery. It improves security and brings a bankable option that highlights growth for your career trajectory. It allows you to take your talents to the next level. It highlights lively discussions and a group environment that grows your skillset. As your abilities rise, it brings unique options to your table. News and excitement ahead make a grand entrance and open the door to progression. It does help you break fresh ground and reach an ambitious goal.

You hear a snippet of information on the wind; it carries news worth investigating and soon connects you with an area that offers learning and growth. It shines a light on advancing your abilities and expanding your skills into new areas. Exploring options jumpstart a path forward towards growth and productivity. It reveals a journey that sees you reaching for goals and expanding your reach. It gives you the chance to reboot the course ahead and chase your dreams. Putting fuel on your creativity's fire sees your passion burning as you advance your vision forward. Change surrounds your life as a new role is on offer soon. A clue ahead reveals a piece to the puzzle. It lets you move steadily towards your vision. Life heads to an upswing: bringing a productive and dynamic environment.

Ursids Meteor Shower. Mercury at Greatest Eastern elongation. Yule/Winter Solstice at week's end. It emphasizes home and family life that ground foundations in a stable environment. It sows the seeds for future progress and brings new possibilities into focus. It gets nourishing energy into your environment that smooths tension and paves the way for a fresh start. Taking time to ground your restless vibes releases the stress and encourages gentle expansion into new areas. It brings the right type of options that let you develop your talents. A sense of manifestation brings intriguing possibilities that help you tap into a curious new assignment.

Communication arrives that brings a breath of fresh air into your environment. It offers a beautiful time of sharing thoughts with another person. This individual has recently reawakened to buried feelings. As their emotions rise to the surface, they become inspired to connect the dots and seek to become closer with you. Serendipity lights the way forward, bringing blessings and lightness into your world. Nourishing the seeds of potential brings expansion to your social life. It draws this person into your inner circle, which encourages a strong foundation in your home life.

DECEMBER WEEK FOUR

New Moon in Capricorn. Mercury Retrograde begins this week. You may be feeling cooped in and restless. Rest assured, you soon find a suitable outlet for your excess energy. It brings a refreshing change of pace that heightens creativity. It's a prime time to look into options of learning and growth. Planning your vision for the future creates a blend of manifestation that sets in motion new goals. It brings a stellar phase of progressing your world and lines up an opportunity worth exploring. It breaks old patterns and ways of thinking; it draws a diverse road of new interests.

Changes surround your situation. It lights your life up across the board with new potential. A sense of connection lets you tap into a broader social environment. Issues and troubles soon wash away under a surge of potential. Improvement may be rapid as you dive into an environment that offers growth. It gives you a chance to flex your talents and develop an area of interest. Investigating new leads uncovers a gem.

You soon resolve a situation that has caused a bitter taste. As the sour note fades, and the memories linger in your mind, letting you learn a lesson for future use. Favorable changes are coming up that draw social engagement. It does connect you with people who offer support and guidance. A big reveal is coming that brings clarity into the path ahead. You glide into a phase of hope, advancement, and potential.

Dear Stargazer,

I hope you have enjoyed planning your year with the stars utilizing Astrology and Zodiac influences. My yearly zodiac books feature a weekly (four weeks to a month) horoscope. You can find me on the sites below where you can get personal astrology or intuitive readings.

https://www.facebook.com/SiaSands

Instagram: SiaSands

You can order an Astrology reading at:

https://psychic-emails.com/

Leaving a review is welcomed and appreciated.

Many Blessings,

Sia Sands